A Rule of St. Nicholas

(How to save you and your family from
a modern Western Christmas)

Suggested by:

Deacon Nathan Gunn

FORWARD:

I have a dream, and I hope that you share the same dream, that somehow, some way, and almost against all odds, the NEXT Christmas will be more meaningful, more joyous, more in keeping with the truth of Christmas than ever before.

Well, after reading Deacon Nathan Gunn's A Rule of St. Nicholas, I have found the perfect ingredients for making it just that – and you will also.

Amazingly, it involves putting St. Nicholas and "his Rule" front and center. I have, for so long, seen "Santa Claus" as the one trying to rob me of the sacredness of Jesus coming upon this earth, when all along the pre-eminent "Santa Claus" brought Jesus front and center in all he did – and so can you when you find out about him in this inspiring work.

Each December, I rejoice in hearing the song – "The Real Meaning of Christmas Is The Giving Of Love Everyday". What! "It's about giving and not receiving?" What! "It is giving something I already have and don't have to buy and its an intangible called Love?" What! "Christmas is not ONE day then we are on to Valentine's Day?"

Nathan Gunn, in his A Rule of St Nicholas has given us a powerful example of how to live our lives in ways that will bring the real joy of Christmas to faces and hearts all year long.

Mohatma Ghandi challenges us to – "Be the change you want to see in our world." What if this Christmas we decided, once and for all time, to celebrate in a way that brings us, and others, happiness all year long? We have the power and A Rule of St. Nicholas has the way!

(Rev. Msgr.) J Robert Yeazel - Retired

A Word about "Rules" and Saints

We may not be entirely familiar with the idea of a "Rule" to govern our lives. Broadly speaking, rules are the written or agreed upon regulations that govern the way an activity or relationship are meant to be conducted. In the narrow sense in the history of Christian communities, a "Rule" were the virtues, habits and customs that made a certain Christian group unique. St Benedict wrote his "Rule" for his monks in 516 and that document organized not only their daily activities but also their spirituality. Rules are usually formed around Saints and their communities moving forward.

As my family and I began to dig into the life of St. Nicholas, I went searching for Rule of St. Nicholas. To my surprise, it didn't exist. While there were volumes and volumes about the life and legend of the Saint, there was no particular spirituality formed around St. Nicholas.

This "Rule" is only "suggested" because I am only a curious Deacon. I have no authority on the matter and there certainly are people better qualified than me to codify an official "Rule". What we have here is my best suggestion based on the history, the stories and what we have seen and experienced. If this goes well, someone else will pick it up and do something wonderful and grand.

While we may be unfamiliar with a "Rule", many of us may also be uncomfortable or unaware of the reality of the Saints. That's ok – I was too. In fact, the stories you'll read were a major part of my learning.

Just to put people at ease – having a relationship with a Saint or asking them for prayer doesn't detract at all from our personal relationship with Jesus and the Holy Spirit. In fact, we've found that knowing St. Nicholas has actually strengthened and deepened that personal faith. The Saints are saints precisely because everything in their lives was about Jesus.

As a minister, people ask me all the time to pray for them. What an honor! I cherish adding them and their burdens to my morning prayer time. Never once have I considered saying to a person in need, "Don't ask me to pray for you – you should only ask Jesus for help." In fact, I've never met anyone who has said that in reply. Instead we enter into that mystical Body of Christ and hold one another's joys, trials and sufferings before the Lord of Hosts. I've learned through experience that the Saints are our best prayer partners – by virtue of their life on earth and the reality of their current life in Heaven.

For the sake of this limited project, have an open mind and lean into the history. And don't forget, St. Paul tells us that we're all called to be saints (1 Cor 1:2) – it probably won't bother us after we're dead if people ask us to help them out a little too.

Introduction

It all began with an ark.

Things were tight back then in our household. We had just bought a house that had been stuck deep in the 1950s and began its renovation. Our oldest son was not yet three years old and our newborn had come in May. We used to pass easy time in the local shopping mall – it provided protection from the harsh Upstate winter winds and allowed our boy to run around freely in the wide empty hallways. There was one particular end of the mall that was both sloped and carpeted and he loved to pitter-patter up and down the thoroughfare.

As Christmas approached, we had put together a modest collection of toys for gifts. While it was less than we desired to lavish on them, they were young and this Christmas would not be frozen in their memory. Still, I had a twinge of sadness and perhaps even wondered at our ability as providers compared against the normal cultural expectations at that season. Besides, I had already joked regularly with my wife that we wouldn't be able to keep the house once we had to pay the Upstate New York taxes that January.

And then it happened. Our little boy, with the big cheeks and the cherub nose, walked right up to the Christmas window of the expensive toy store. You know the type of store? It's the one that has the toys from England. The ones where the dolls all have names and their clothes cost more than my clothes – or my wife's clothes. I'm not sure how we let it happen – we never went actually *into* that store, but our boy was drawn to that window with a focus that we not yet seen in him.

He got his face right up to the glass and lingered for a while. And then, without turning his head away from the glass, he said to me — clear as day,

"That's it Daddy. That's what you can get me for Christmas. That ark."

You see, our son loved animals. And when I say he loved animals, you got an idea in your mind, but it was wrong — he loved them much, much more than you're thinking. And this toy, this ark — this was no ordinary set. This was the Playmobil Noah's Ark complete with 5-6 pairs of animals, a working winch, a ramp, removable living quarters and birds. This set even came with Noah... and his wife. It was the dream Noah's ark.

"That's it Daddy. That's what you can get me for Christmas. That ark."

Who wouldn't want that ark? I wanted that ark! I was spellbound as well. It was so clean, so crisp, so cool. As my eyes gazed over the set, I imagined the hours of joy my boys would have with those animals. It even floated! And best of all — it was even a Biblical toy!

As my eyes moved across the display, I scanned slowly and carefully to the upper left-hand corner. This was the dreaded space for me... the place of price tags. I knew it would be bad — this was the expensive toy store. But I couldn't believe it when the tag read-

$99.

You have to understand. Things were tight in our house. Not public assistance tight, but I hadn't spent $100 on my wife for anything since our honeymoon. I hadn't even considered the possibility of a day where I would have $100 to spend on anyone I loved. And yet – there it was. I looked down at my boy and he looked at me – smiling. Joyful. Expectant. He had never asked for anything before. I guess he decided to go big. But he was right. That ark was awesome.

The date was December 21st.

That night, I struggled within myself. I was a good dad. My wife was the best mom I knew – by a lot. I knew that materialism and consumerism were wrong and we had pledged to orient our lives differently. We were making it work and yet at the same time – how could I possibly make this work? I was frustrated. Frustrated with my income and frustrated with my inability to make this happen for my sons. I did have different connections to make a little bit more money from time to time, but there was nothing I could do in such a quick turnaround.

Nothing happened December 22nd.

Then on December 23rd, I went out on our front porch to grab my shovel and clear the walk of snow when I discovered a simple envelope with no name in front of the door. Our porch is enclosed so it was safe from the elements. It was morning. There were no tracks in the snow. If had been dropped off by someone, they were long gone.

I reached down and picked up the envelope and opened it hastily. The card inside was a beautiful lithograph of Noah's Ark. It wasn't a fancy painting, nor a child's rendition, but a simple, well-done painting of the famous scene.

When I opened the card, the message was simple. It read:

"With faith, Noah built the ark."

Next to that message, folded-up, were 5 crisp $20 bills.

I ran inside and showed my wife the card and its contents and asked her if she had told anyone. With tears in her eyes, she said she kept to herself – besides – who walks around telling their friends they can't buy their kid what they want for Christmas?

That day I rushed off to that expensive toy store – it was my only visit across its threshold. I bought that ark for my boy and he opened it on Christmas morning. He hugged us tight and we played with that thing, not for hours, not for days, but for years.

Little did I know, that little card with $100 was the first breadcrumb. St Nicholas had visited our family and he was wooing us to himself. Slow as I am, it took a while for me to figure out who was pulling the strings and what the message was, but once we began to follow the path, it became clear and fast-moving. He had used my boy to gain our family.

The Rule of St. Nicholas

Be Generous

Love Children

Stand for the Truth

Work for Justice

Live with Joy

The First Rule

Be Generous

St Nicholas is generous.

His legend starts with 3 bags of gold. You've probably heard
the story. Nicholas was Bishop of Myra. He was born in
270 and died in 342. Stories point to Nicholas being present
at the First Council of Nicaea in 325 which means he was
made Bishop before that. During his time as Bishop, he
became aware of a father who was struggling to make ends meet.
This particular father had 3 daughters and had decided that in
order to make ends meet, he would need to sell his oldest
daughter into marriage. The maiden had a boyfriend but
apparently the young couple couldn't get staked out on their
own.

The family's plight got back to Nicholas and he had compassion
on them. At night, well after people had gone to bed, the Saint
snuck through the city and found the open window of the
family's home. Wishing to remain anonymous, Nicholas threw
a bag of gold coins through the window and then snuck back to
his home.

Legend speaks of the father waking up and discovering a bag of
gold, at the bottom of the stockings that had been hung by the
chimney to dry out. Overjoyed, he took the gift and gave it to
his daughter who married her boyfriend and they started out on
their own.

As fate would have it, our original family continued to fall on
hard times and the father decided to put his second daughter up

for a dowry. The word got back to Nicholas and he repeated his late night excursion and tossed another sack of gold into the family's open window. Overjoyed, the father set his daughter up with her boyfriend and a new family was created.

Apparently, things were tough in Myra and our father was unable to lift himself out of poverty. Shamefully, he decided to put his third daughter out to the highest suitor. Nicholas came to the rescue again but as he snuck away, the father was ready and chased him throughout the streets of Myra. After a long chase, the father caught up with the Saint and immediately, upon recognizing the Bishop repented of his decision and pledged to set his life in a new direction.

I can remember learning of this episode for the first time and chuckling a bit at the narrative; trying to discern what was real and what was legend. And that is the crux of St. Nicholas. St. Nicholas is real. He lived, he died. He was active and he was known as the "Wonderworker." Whether the Bishop of Myra in the 3rd or 4th century *actually* pitched gold sacks into open windows is a question lost to history, but what is real is that millions and millions of people place stockings at their fireplaces and millions and millions of other people place their shoes outside their doors — all with the expectation that someone will fill them up; and they get filled!

I remember wrestling with this idea that there is a foggy line with St. Nicholas between legend and real when we drove through Las Vegas a few years ago. We were doing a southwest family Spring Break trip. Phoenix with friends. Good Friday and Easter in Sedona. Grand Canyon. Bryce Canyon and Mt. Zion. We were ending our time with friends in Disneyland so we decided to break-up our drive with a night

in Las Vegas. Our boys loved the show "Pawn Stars" and we thought it'd be cool to go in the actual store from TV and check things out.
We rolled into town and parked the car near the store, stood in line and made it in before filming began. And that's when I saw it. Just as my boys were about to meet (a bonfire TV celebrity at the time) – my eyes were fixated on the logo for the show:

World Famous Gold and Silver Pawn Shop.

And between the words Famous and Gold were three hanging gold balls. St Nicholas is the patron saint of pawnbrokers – I suppose because he traded up with those 3 bags of gold – bringing freedom and life to the family. But what was more stunning to me was that I was sitting in Las Vegas Nevada – nearly 7,000 miles from Myra Turkey – roughly 1600 years after the story took place and there they were – the three golden balls.

With St. Nicholas, there's an amazing blending of legend and history. But the remnants of his life and his stories are all-around us. And it began to dawn on me. If he could throw bags of gold through windows, he could slip envelopes of cash onto my porch.

For the next several Decembers, anonymous envelopes of cash began to land on our porch. For the first year or two, it was exactly what we needed for that something "extra" that we couldn't afford for the boys at Christmas. It started with the kids and the gifts. We were slow to pick-up on it. We just weren't adept at reading the signs.

There was the year that the Lego Imperial Star Destroyer came out before the holiday. It had 1366 pieces and a special chamber where Darth Vader got shaved. Feel free to laugh – but it was so cool that I wanted it. Once again – no way. Way beyond our budget. But then, the funds started showing up. Not always in envelopes, but cash here, cash there – until we realized. We had the exact amount needed to bless the boys with the set.

Now at this point you're probably thinking that I'm not a very spiritual person. I mean here's a guy getting anonymous cash in the season of Advent and I'm buying up high-end expensive toys for my kids and not even considering giving it to the poor and needy at Christmas. And you're totally right. I wasn't there yet – the Saint was wooing me. My wife and I were givers and we tithed to both Church and Charities but being tight, we were limited. We never conceived of the idea of extra giving or being in a place to ever do "more". We possessed the heart, but not the dough.

But then things began to change. We realized that we were raising boys in an environment where everything was about the next glitzy toy, the next tech gadget, the next gaming system. Not only could we not keep up – we didn't want to. Our motto for raising kids was simple –

"If everyone else is doing it – do the opposite"

St Paul tells the young church in Rome: "Do not conform any longer to the pattern of the world but be transformed by the renewing of your mind" (Rom 12:2). Simply put – if you're not sure what to do – look at what everyone is doing and go in the opposite direction. This simple approach to parenting began to really serve us well.

And that's when the Parish Giving Tree kicked in.

Every year to kick off Advent, our large parish took names from needy folks in the community and beyond and put the names and needs on the "Giving Tree" in the gathering area outside the sanctuary on the first Sunday of Advent. 2 weeks later, at all 4 Masses, streams of families came back with hundreds of brightly decorated presents for people they had never met. Both our boys were in the Parish school by this point and we got the idea: what if we did the Giving Tree as a family. As we talked more about it, we decided to tie it into December 6th – the Feast Day of St Nicholas. Now understand, we didn't yet know St. Nicholas nor that it was him dropping cash on our porch, but we saw his name right on the calendar between 1st Sunday of Advent and the return date for the gifts. We came up with a plan.

On the first Sunday of Advent, we'd let the boys pick tags. Then on December 6th we'd go to Kohls and Target and have them pick out the presents. We'd celebrate with dinner at Red Robin (unlimited steak fries – I was still cheap) and then go home to wrap them all up. The whole thing was made even better when some of our best friends and their 4 kids decided to work a classroom with us on the Gift Return Day.

But then something went wrong.

Our boys were both generous and fiscally irresponsible.

They grabbed about 8 tags. They looked for kids that were similar to themselves with gifts they would like. They were looking for kids they could relate to. They loved it. And then it got worse. My younger son told us that his teacher was doing a collection for socks for the homeless so when we went to Target we needed to get some of those too.

My wife and I began to sweat it. As we walked around Target on December 6th, the boys got in the giving spirit. I'll never forget my boy holding a 10 pack and 20 pack of socks and saying – "Which one is better?" –

"What do you think?" I responded.

Then he smiled and said, "Both!"

And both went sailing into my cart.

At the end of Target, we let our oldest swipe the credit card.

$350.

Then off to Kohls.

We let the younger one swipe the card:

$250. (at least we got the Kohl's cash)

The boys thought this was the greatest night ever. Our van was full of packages and toys and socks and their bellies were full of steak fries. What could possibly be better?

The only issue was – I didn't have $600 or anywhere close to that to cover the bill. A smart buddy of mine who was a great financial planner had told me that I needed to get $10,000 saved up as a first goal towards fiscal health. At this point in my life, we didn't have $1000 saved – let alone in my checking account month to month. Everything was about living in the present moment and I remember going to sleep that night thinking I've got the happiest boys in the world and they're they most generous chaps you could ever find – but now Lord Jesus – someone's got to pay for this.

And then it began again. Not in one lump – but almost in payments. It was goofy. I recall one friend literally meeting me for lunch and stuffing an envelope in my pocket. He was a generous friend but he had never done anything like that before. I came home and opened it –

$500.

By Christmas Eve we had over $1600 given to us in cash payments – from friends or anonymous stashes that would appear. Somehow – we were in the black on the whole thing and our family could move forward. And that's when I decided to get more serious about this St. Nicholas thing.

We had chosen December 6th as a way to avert our children's gaze from the huge haul of gifts and consumerism with cultural Christmas. We had hoped that by focusing on giving to those in need, perhaps we'd avoid the pitfalls of materialism and trying ourselves to make sure that we were providing "enough". The whole idea of generosity as an anecdote to materialism wasn't anything new — but discovering the figure of St. Nicholas at the center of the "discipline" turned out to be the best gift of all.

Generosity wasn't something we moved towards reluctantly, we just needed to be mentored or brought along. Learning that there was a figure who had given so much for the needs of others — especially for a family in need provided both direction and inspiration. And learning that the symbols — those three gold balls — had traveled through time and space made the whole discipline something even more potent.

As I spent the year researching about the Saint, other characteristics began to emerge and new ideas came to mind about how we might celebrate December 6th. We decided to up the ante.

The next year, we had newlyweds as neighbors. We worked with the wife and the husband was someone we had known since he as in high school. This was their first year married. Michael was a Veteran of a tour in Afghanistan and was spending the holiday serving for the Guard down in Louisiana- helping to bring soldiers back into the population after their own tours.

Michael had strict word that he would be working Christmas Eve and there was no reason for Eileen to imagine that she could spend the holiday with him. When it came to December 6th, out we headed with the tags: Target — Kohl's — Red Robin. The kids had a grand time and we had a van overflowing with packages for the Giving Tree. When we got to Red Robin — we talked with the boys about our friends' situation and we agreed to ask St. Nicholas to help. I told them that I would set aside — in my mind — an amount of money that would be the uncomfortable amount of money that Eileen wouldn't want to spend to buy herself a last minute ticket to Louisiana.

We told Eileen that we had St. Nicholas working on her dilemma and we waited. In my mind, I had set aside $250 to offer her because I figured as newlyweds, they'd pay $400 to get a ticket for Christmas together, but not $650 – and a last minute ticket all the way down to Louisiana would cost at least that much.

Weeks went by and no call from Michael. And then it came. Around December 20th, Eileen came over – VERY excited. She said –

"You're not going to believe this! Michael's commander gave him Christmas Eve and Christmas Day off. I'm free to head down to be with him for the holiday. The only problem was that the ticket is more than I wanted to spend.. But then my mom called. Now my mom doesn't know anything about this. My mom called just to tell me that a refund from the wedding came in and she was mailing me a check – guess how much it's for?"

I said – "$250."

She said "Yeah!! How'd you know!"

My wife and I just looked at each other – we had been out-foxed – out maneuvered – out-given. You see – we had already received the money for December 6th- Giving Tree Night and we had also received the money for Eileen's ticket – the extra $250. We had more than we needed even though we were trying to be generous – AND – our friend was getting exactly what she wanted.

This was about when we began to understand that we were being led down a path of very large bread crumbs. Generosity was something much, much larger than we had imagined. The virtue wasn't simply about giving to those in need although that is the core. The second layer of giving to those who can't or won't give back to you was so freeing from expectations. But this was a new dimension – this was tapping into a deposit of resources we were not familiar with.

Each season – we had been giving away toys and gifts and clothes with money we had not yet received. Only to receive more than we had given away. With our neighbors' story – we were taken out as the middle men – the money and the blessing had gone straight to them and we still had more than we started with. There was a stream of gold bags that never ended... what started as an envelope with 5 twenties on our porch had just sent our neighbor to Louisiana for Christmas with her new husband.

That's the beauty of generosity as an alternative lifestyle. So much of disengaging from the world or being counter-cultural requires simplicity and reduction – all virtuous. If we truly are not going to conform to the "patterns of the world" then we can get by with much less. Consumerism needs to be met with a vigilant "no" to the incessant advertising and messaging. False idols promising fulfillment abound and cutting them out of our lives is a profound gift and challenge.

And yet – we are still raising families, still living in communities, still engaging this culture. Unless we're called to live "off the grid" or to become an ascetic, we still need to forge a way forward. How can we live in any culture and push back against the norm for "more" without replacing that space with something? Our family was being taught that the space created by resisting the pressure of the world was filled by generosity. And the space wasn't just filled – it was over-flowing.

There is a resolution in resisting materialism. A firm and convicted stance; that is the first step in repenting from that portion of the idolatry of our culture. But repentance, true change, offers a second step – a new direction. For us, that direction was following Santa Claus into joyful generosity.

St. Paul writes his bumbling friends in Corinth about this opportunity in generosity:

"Each of you should give what you have decided in your heart to give, not reluctantly or under compulsion, for God loves a cheerful giver. And God is able to bless you abundantly, so that in all things at all times, having all you need, you will abound in every good work. As it is written, 'They have freely scattered their gifts to the poor; their righteousness endures forever" (2 Corinthians 9: 6-9).

At face value, Paul is encouraging a generous lifestyle. On deeper analysis, we learn that Paul is talking about an attitude as well. The original Greek word for "cheerful" is *hilaros*. *Hilaros* is our root for *hilar*ious. Consider that – when was the last time we attended a fundraiser for a charity we love or a school our kids attend – or the last time a Girl Scout came to our doors to sell her cookies and we and the community responded with hilarious giving. Giving that says, "Yes! I'm so glad you asked! What do you need? Here's more!".

It almost takes practice saying those phrases out loud. I remember talking over generosity with my good friend and mentor Monsignor Yeazel. Fr Bob helped me come to the realization that when someone actually takes the time to ask me to support them – it's a compliment! Not only do they think I have money – but they think I care enough for them to part with it! Hilarious giving encourages us to "scatter our gifts freely". There is no shortage of opportunities! There is no way that the compelling places of need will run out before our money does.

So what does Hilarious Giving translate to in a real dollars and sense form?

I was (and am) a rabid budgeter. I wasn't always that way, but starting out, we were the couple who would have our shopping list on the back of an envelope and I kept track with a pencil and we were the ones who ran out of the weekly budget somewhere between cereal and toilet paper. (Forget the freezer section and the ice cream).

So when St. Nicholas got ahold of us, we took some notes.

To our disgust, payments on interest on our mortgage and our property taxes were the #1 and #2 things we spent our money on each year. Pathetic. Paying a bank for the privilege to live in our house and the government for the privilege to live in our town were not in-line with Hilarious Giving. We set a goal and within two years – those items began to move down on our list. As our income went up, we kept our expenses down and allowed for our Giving to outpace our debt and our taxes. It took discipline and it took time. We made monthly pledges to causes we adored, mostly around children and we looked for other opportunities to give out of pocket. But here is the shocker –

3, 4, 5 years in – all of a sudden our savings grew too. As we learned to "freely scatter our gifts to the poor" we tapped into something much larger. Sure we had our jobs and our income. But there was another bucket of money from somewhere else that just continued to bless our lives. Ironically, our boys became teenagers and all-of-a-sudden feeding them and their friends became a top-5 expense. Savings for college and cars and all the other experiences that a young family has caused our budget to remain a juggling act at times, but Hilarious Generosity had freed our hearts from being slaves to the culture and worshipping the idols of materialism and consumerism.

In his Sermon on the Mount, Jesus invites us into a healthier and liberating relationship with both materialism and anxiety. He reminds us of the way in the which the birds of the air and the lilies of the field are provided for (Matt 6) and then exhorts us to place our own faith squarely in the provision of God our Father. Jesus challenges us to be different than that "pagans" who run after worrisome things but instead, to live in quiet and hopeful confidence that God will provide. True freedom comes from detaching from this world of material consumption and acquisition and living faith-filled lives centered around generosity.

To be a follower of St. Nicolas, one has to practice hilarious generosity.

The Second Rule

Love Children

St. Nicolas loves children.

We've heard the story of the father and his daughters, but St. Nicholas didn't stop there. Let's remember that he is SAINT Nicholas, so he kept doing his good works after he was dead. I know that's a stretch for our modern sensibilities, but it turns out to be more common than you'd think for the class of Saints.

Years after St. Nicholas had died, the town of Myra was preparing for the celebration of St. Nicholas Day. On the very eve of the celebration, a band of pirates happened into the city and began to loot the town. Along with the silver and gold they stole from the Saint's very own Church, they left with a little boy named Basilious.

As one would expect, Basilious' parents were beside themselves with worry and spent the year in agony. Basilious himself became the cupbearer for the emir of the marauders. Day after day, he served in the royal chambers of the people's leader. As the one-year anniversary of Basilious' capture approached, the boy's parents decided to stay home, away from the celebrations and to pray quietly to the Saint for their boy. Likewise, as Basillious served the emir that fateful night, he appeared distraught. Upon questioning, the boy revealed his sadness at being separated from his family and the celebration of St. Nicholas Day at home. As he approached the ruler with his golden cup, Basilious was whisked away. Terrified at first, he was comforted by the presence of St. Nicholas himself who delivered the boy to his parents – still holding the golden chalice of the emir! Imagine the celebration in ancient Myra the next day when Basillious and his family were restored!

Admittingly, this story dovetails with another virtue connected to St. Nicholas but the narrative centers around his holy activities with children. Again, we have to remind ourselves that we're talking about the space where history meets legend. When we consider the person of Santa Claus, we immediately turn to the figure at Christmas and the wild generosity shown to billions of kids around the world.

Consider for a second – is there any figure in the history of the world more closely associated with the pure love of children than Santa Claus? Now we can admit, as mature adults, that the modern-day use and image of Santa Claus does not imbody nor reflect the magnificence of the Saint in totality nor perfectly – but this part they got right – to be devoted to St Nicholas, to reflect his life and direction, a person has to keep pace with the love of children.

At first glance, this seemed easy. We had two kids and as long was we loved those stinkers, we'd be in good shape. Of course, loving your own kids or grandkids is a great place to start and a non-negotiable. But following a Saint isn't about doing what's expected. As our devotion grew, opportunities grew as well.

Not long after we moved into that new house we couldn't afford to even remodel, we met our dear neighbors, the Parkers. We didn't know that they would become two of our dearest friends over the next decades, but their two kids were close in age to ours so we began to journey together. Soon after our second boy could walk, their kids needed a place to be during the day while the parents worked. Tammy had already been trained and worked in multiple environments professionally with kids before she "stayed home" with our own. Knowing that the Parkers could use a hand, she offered to have the Parker kids at our house each day at a huge discount from normal day-care rates.

Following St. Nicholas doesn't mean that everyone should open their home as a neighborhood discount day-care, but it does mean that we can remain soft and open to ways in which we can open our doors to kids and provide good and safe places for them.

Not long after the boys started school, a different opportunity arose – the local Little League. I loved baseball and outside of my family and work, nothing had captured my heart and imagination like baseball had. As our oldest entered into T-Ball, I joined the ranks of Little League coaches. For the next 10 years of my life, there was little that brought me more joy than running Little League teams in our town for kids 12 and under.

Now these are things that normal people do: watch the neighbor's kids and coach in youth sports. But there's a difference with St. Nicholas. There is a manner in which a person opens their home and a manner is which a person coaches another person's kid that changes everything.

When you think of Santa Claus – what picture do you have?

Smiling? Happy? Joyful?

Do you hear… "He was so jolly and plump, a right jolly o' jolly o' elf"?

Joy – happiness – friendliness – laughter.

Believe it or not, these are not the typical experiences of kids in Day Care or youth sports, let alone the majority of things that are centered around kids anymore. In fact, as most young people navigate their path to adulthood, most of the extra activities they engage with add to their stress and misery as a result of the adults who lead them. St Nicholas would have had none of that.

As we dipped our toes into engaging our kids and other children in our community, we saw an opportunity to spread joy and happiness. The irony was that by treating kids and families with an upbeat and joyful spirit, we were somehow being counter-cultural. We were once again reminded of St. Paul's admonition to the Roman church: "Do not conform any longer to the patterns of this world but be transformed by the renewing of your mind" (Romans 12:2). This might seem a bit dramatic, but engaging the extracurricular activities in your community with kids and using the foundational principle of the experience of the child as opposed to his or her performance or achievement was in fact against the patterns of this high-pressured world.

We've all read about the horrific rates of depression, anxiety and even suicide among young people. There is a complex myriad of reasons behind this sociological and psychological phenomenon. Young people, especially in the developed western world have never had access to so much – perhaps too much! Yet in the midst of unfettered access to so much possibility, our young people are suffering like never before recorded. This juxtaposition dovetails with an early legend of St. Nicolas.

How did the Saint begin to get so closely associated with children? This is a unique connection when we think of the Hall of Fame of the Saints – consider again, is there another figure in human history so closely associated with children as St. Nicholas and Santa Claus?

An ancient manuscript has been discovered from the 11th century that sources from a school in Germany. The manuscripts contains a story in the form of play. In this play, three young men, possibly religious men in formation take up lodging for the night at an inn. As the innkeeper and his wife see their money bag, they hatch the plan to murder them and steal their bag. Having murdered the travelers, their evening is interrupted by a visitor at the door – none other than St Nicholas!

As the story goes on, Nicholas disguises himself as a poor beggar and asks the couple for some meat. The innkeeper and his wife tell the Saint that they are out of food and the disguised beggar responds in a rhyming (in Latin) stanza that accuses the couple of not only lying to him, but also of killing the 3 young men. There aren't details about the couple's reaction but St. Nicholas prays for forgiveness and raises the young men from the dead. The story ends with a worship chorus of thanksgiving to both God and our hero, St. Nicholas.

What is so significant about this fable? Remember, with St. Nicholas, we are talking about the blend of history and legend. This story was performed as a play throughout the region and is one of the earliest recorded plays in the Middle Ages that is neither Biblical nor liturgical in nature. As the play was retold and modified for school audiences, the young seminarians become young children. Oftentimes this play was performed in that period on the eve of St. Nicholas Day – a day already associated with gifts of candy and fruit given in children's shoes in honor of the life-saving actions of Nicholas in Myra. As time went on, in order to keep the audience's attention, the murders of the children often turned to dismemberment and the grotesque detail of the kid's portions being salted in a pickle barrel. Over the centuries, one central figure and action remained the same – St. Nicholas emerges and saves the kids – raising them back to life.

It's easy to imagine a small group of children, or perhaps even a gathering of a village in a square on the evening of December 5th. Torches lit the night air and minstrel music could be heard. Delicious smells from cooked meats and the satisfaction of knowing that the next day was a day away from work and dedicated to the memory of a benevolent Saint who protected children. In the midst of the laughter and merriment – a true "night off" for the townspeople, players take to a small stage and tell the story of St. Nicholas and his saving actions. Thwarting the evil innkeeper and his wife and preserving the lives of 3 boys whom had fallen victim to some adults' terrible scheme.

As this fable and the festivities linked to St. Nicholas Day developed across centuries, it is no wonder that such an easy connection was seared into the consciousness of a continent. And it is important to pause and ask – If not St. Nicholas, then who? Who steps into that void – that place of joy, safety and comfort? Who else would receive millions of letters – even today! Even in today's scientific and mechanized world where we are told that faith and reason cannot meet – who is there today that can remain a hero figure and capture the hearts of young people on such a personal level? Kids don't write letters to Iron Man. Black Panther is a great hero but he's not going to show up at your house and nobody expects Spiderman to know the names of every kid on the planet. Long before we had comic books and westerns and fantasy heroes to distract us from the darkness of our every day world, people had St. Nicholas and time and time again, he saved the children from their peril.

What connections can we make?

Our kids today are like those poor unsuspecting travelers. Let's hope they don't end up in a pickle barrel, but in a very real sense, our own children are on their own journey and oftentimes, the very people and places that are intended for their refreshment and safety end up being the sources of pain, sorrow, anxiety and on occasion, death itself.

Young people are fantastically resilient but in many instances, the odds are stacked against them. Consider the dramatic and oftentimes tragic childhoods of so many of children who grow in cities, developing nations or war-torn environments. Many young people enter into adolescence already dismembered emotionally, mentally and spiritually as a result of abuse, neglect or poverty. So many young people's youth is stolen from them by the horrific actions of adults, family members or authority figures. For those young people who were blessed to navigate childhood unscathed by the scarring actions of others, most enter into a system designed by the world that seeks to evaluate and promote those who are able to achieve and produce. Even the very activities that are meant to distract or soften the strain of school and work end up creating a new layer of pressure and anxiety. Over all of this backdrop, young people themselves torture one another over social media and are exposed to the full legion of evil that unfettered access to the internet can bring. All of this spinning culminates with one cultural promise and expectation — attending a college one can't afford to discover "who you really are" while racking up debilitating debt that gets paid off over a lifetime. Its no wonder that so many young people self-medicate through alcohol and substance abuse, bullying, self-mutilation and worse.

In reality, kids haven't changed. If anything, the western world has more to offer them than at any point in human history and yet, the constructs of our societies have created more misery and pain than at any other point. What does St. Nicholas offer as an anecdote to such a system?

As we reflect on the three stories — the daughters, the boys and our kidnapped servant boy- we see the same themes emerge.

Safety. Protection. Healing. A person devoted to St. Nicholas works to create safe spaces for kids. Whether this be in your own home, at the ball field, at the playground, in the grocery store — this person is on the lookout for opportunities to expand safe places for kids. At the same time, we adopt a broad view of safety that includes the emotional, mental and spiritual dimensions of young people. We don't allow ourselves to be fooled by the healthy-looking young person when we know the possibility exists of a soul that's in ruins. As we consider young people from a holistic perspective, our expectations of ourselves and our community need to change. As we step into positions of influence for the sake of young people, we run things and exert influence with the whole person in mind. Things like winning and losing or the development of skills or passing on the last local gossip lose their luster when a follower of St Nicholas sees the opportunity to protect and nurture the interior space of a developing young person. Things like winning, losing, practicing and developing skills become tools instead of goals.

St Nicholas intervened for the sake of kids and brought healing and restoration into their lives and families. A person dedicated to St. Nicholas views their position as parent, neighbor, teacher, counselor, youth minister, small business owner – through the lens of expanding the space for safety and healing for young people in the community. While always keeping a primary focus on our families, we take an active role to prioritize the protection of kids and work to bring healing into their lives.

It would be worth surveying the landscape of both ancient and modern super heroes. As we look across the myriad of figures, would we find anyone in Greek lore or that shows up on the blockbuster screens of today that makes the safety and restoration of children a primary *modus oporundi*? Is there any other figure that drew villagers together for centuries to regale the tales of the kids he had saved? Is there another hero that received the aspirations and affections of the children of the world across the millennia? Is there another Saint so closely associated with devotion to kids?

To follow St. Nicolas, one has to love and protect kids.

The Third Rule

Stand for the Truth

St Nicholas lived during interesting times – and that's putting it mildly. When he accepted his call to ministry and leadership as a Bishop, Christianity was outlawed and a vow to Christ was a vow against Caesar which would land someone in jail and sometimes on a cross or in an arena. But by the time Nicholas died, Christianity was on its way to being the state religion and the centuries-old pagan idols were on the run. The Saint lived in a transitionary time and a time when the very notion of sacred truths about Christ and worship where up-for-grabs. Without a doubt, each era presents its challenges and no person gets off easily. We must all grapple with truth and the very idea of universals. As we read these lines today, we live in a post-Christian time where relativism and individualism are not only valued and promoted, they are now generationally imbedded. As long as people have been able to reflect on their lives and existence, curiosity and wonder alone have caused people to contemplate and argue great questions about life. It would be without merit to say that today is harder than yesterday or more difficult than when St. Nicholas was alive. Yet, we can identify that Santa Claus was alive during a very volatile time when outcomes where unknown and concepts were being created. There were active arguments and friendships and family ties that were threatened. There was terrible rhetoric and there were cultural icons that came into question. There were traditional rituals that were challenged and there were new ways of operating being introduced.

Essential to this moment was the very identity of the person of Christ and the pagan culture of worship that existed in the world. History and legend teach us that St Nicholas was a bold participant in the drama. Where false teaching and false practices existed, he was present and passionately made his argument – oftentimes proclaiming a truth that the majority did not want to hear.

The major controversy of Nicholas's lifetime centered around the person of Jesus Christ as the Son of God. Without delving into a Master's level conversation, simply stated- for centuries, Christians had taught that Jesus was the Son of God – the Second person in the three Person Trinitarian God. Jesus has unique qualities in that as Son of God He became incarnate through the Virgin Mary and was made one with humanity. Early in the 4th Century, a priest from Alexandria (the philosophical center of the world) challenged his local Church authority by claiming that though Jesus was divine, He could not have always existed since He was "Son" and that only the "Father" could have always existed. Therefore, the Son Jesus was created by God (the Father). This concept of Jesus' nature was controversial and took the name Arianism – after its lead evangelizer Arius. As a major theological fracture developed, the Roman Emperor Constantine intervened. Constantine was on his own spiritual journey, but he was Roman Emperor first which meant he wanted unity. He called together all the Bishops of the Roman world for the first ever world-wide (catholic) Conference – the Council of Nicaea in 325.

While some other lesser matters (when to celebrate Easter for example) were dealt with early on, a rigorous debate broke out regarding Arias and his position. The argument lasted for days and in the end, the orthodox or traditional position of Christ's divine Sonship with the Trinity crafted a new way to express its truth: *homoiousia*. This nifty Greek compound word allowed the Bishops to say – "of one being with" or "consubstantial". In essence – they came up with a new way of saying that although Jesus was a Person of the Son of God in relation to God the Father, He was also one being with – or one substance with God Himself. We hear this truth resonate with "God from God, Light from Light, True God from True God." At the end of the day, this new expression captured the essence of their meaning and Arianism lost the day. What degree Nicholas played in the proceedings is a matter of history and legend.

Nicholas certainly was no Arian; he came down squarely on the side of the orthodox understanding of Jesus and His Divinity. One account of the Council paints Nicholas as being persuasive as a result of his gentleness and holiness to the point of converting the Bishop of Nicaea to his point of view. Another account speaks about the volatility of the Council and Nicholas' passion boiling over to the point of slapping or punching someone with a dissenting position. That story goes on to say that Nicholas was jailed and defrocked for his behavior (slapping people at religious councils is bad form). During the night of his imprisonment, the story goes that the Virgin Mary and Jesus Himself visited the Saint and returned his stole around his shoulders and gave him the Book of the Gospels. Thankfully, Constantine had seen the same vision and Bishop Nicholas was restored to the Council.

Whichever version is true – Nicholas as gentle holy man or Nicholas as passionate rabble-rouser – the story remains that our St Nicholas was present and participating in what may be the most important theological meeting in the history of the world AND that our Bishop Nicholas stood on the side of revealed truth against a strong movement to lessen the person of Christ in the world and the Church. One of the wonderful fruits of the

Council of Nicaea is the word *homoiousia* – a new phrasing of a centuries old idea: Truth hadn't changed, but ways of expressing it had. Another prodigious fruit of the Council was the Nicene Creed itself, which modified slightly again with the Council of Constantinople (381) is perhaps the longest lasting unifying statement of faith in the world. Across thousands of cultures and hundreds of languages and thousands of years, the truth put forth by the Nicene Creed has stood through every test thrown at it. It is hard to imagine any other statement other than the Shema ("Hear O Israel, the Lord your God is One") creating so much unity and singularity of faith. And while the Shema remains the centering creedal statement for the Jewish faith, the Nicene Creed exists beyond cultures, ethnic groups, continents and language. Taken together, they are quite a pair.

So what does Nicholas' involvement with the Council of Nicaea and the crafting of a philosophical argument against Arianism have to do with us?

Standing for the truth means that as people of faith devoted to his way of living, we are not given a free pass in the arguments of the day. Every era has false teachings. Sometimes these teachings touch to the very person of Christ – the center of faith. More often, false teachings center around "new" understandings of the Scriptures and cultural updates of accepted truths. Each culture and era takes a bite out of words and concepts adding layers of meaning or hollowing out meaning entirely.

Take as a simple example – Jesus defined friendship as "Greater love has no one than this, that you lay down your life for your friend" (Jn 13:37). Facebook defined "friend" as a "click" on a box on a screen. Think of the way that beauty has been redefined and scraped of meaning by the beauty industry – what is the contrast of a sunset at the beach with the airbrushed and heavily edited face of a model in an advertisement. Seen in this way – there are endless ways in which today's world seeks to attack or alter truth. Within that last decade, Time magazine printed a cover, boldly asking, "Is Truth Dead?" This cover was meant as a homage to its cover from decades before: "Is God Dead?" but in one sense, both covers ask the same question. So how did we end up in an era where one can universally question universal truth?

At the center of this movement is relativism – a philosophy borne several generations ago which told everyone that there is no universal (ultimate) truths but only that which a person decides or dictates. This modern-day "no-authority / no rules" philosophy is really just a manifestation or a re-write of William of Ockham's 700 year old thoughts of nominalism. Ockham taught that universals were mere concepts and unattached to concrete realities. His writings and teachings led-way to massive fractures in the philosophical and theological world and paved the way for Machiavelli, Spinoza, Descartes and even Luther and Calvin. While Nicholas battled Arias, the long-term argument that entrenches everything today is nominalistic relativism – there are no universal truths and my truth or my version of the truth is all that is needed or necessary. Seen in this way, there is a fracture or disconnection between beliefs and reality.

On face value, the idea that we should all be accepting of one another's opinions, whims and convictions regarding life and its deeper meaning seems charitable. Unfortunately, when we accept that truth is in "the eye of the beholder" not only do we escalate ourselves to the place of God – we actually enter in a world of self-contradiction where no truth can exist at all. Relativism is a house of cards that falls on itself almost immediately. See how simple this is:

If I tell you that your truth is yours and my truth is mine and there is no universal truth, the statement I just made claims to be universally true. Did you see that inherent contradiction? In order for me to accept that everyone's truth can be of equal legitimacy, then I have to accept that really no one's convictions are true. In the world of the ancients, philosophers and theologians took their cues from the natural world. There are natural truths (regardless of whether we like it not) and every day our lives naturally conform to those physical truths. I may want to deny the existence of gravity or the reality of a 4,000 calorie a day diet, but my feet don't leave the ground and when I stuff my face, I get fat. There are natural relationships to natural truths and typically, they don't contradict themselves but battle with one another until one truth naturally supersedes another.

In this same manner, before Ockham and relativists, people would look to the philosophical or spiritual world through the lens of "natural revelation." What principles exist in the natural world that may have a mirror or parallel process in the unseen world of thoughts, ethics and spirituality. One of the most damaging consequences of living in a relativistic world is living in disconnection with the foundational laws of nature and existence. We can see this fractured relationship between nature and self-conceptualization spiraling out-of-control in our modern western world.

The entire absurdity of relativism is seen when we talk about identifying or naming things. If a kid in Kindergarten tells his teacher that the yellow square is a blue triangle for him – why do we tell him he's wrong? If the parents schedule a meeting with the principal and threaten to sue because the school is corrupting his right to individual expression of his truth, how do we think that would go? In fact, our naming of objects points to the concept of universal truth. Consider how many languages exist in the world today and yet, we are able to have consistent translation across those hundreds of languages because if I draw a simple chair on a piece of paper and person speaking Chinese sees that simple image, they can tell me what the word is for "chair" in Chinese because there is a *universal* concept of chair. Imagine if a person simply decided that for them, the word "chair" was attached to the reality of "table" – there would be absolutely no way for them to live in any type of meaningful relationship as the process moved forward.

In 2016, Oxford Dictionaries chose "post-truth" as its international word of the year. What does this mean? Living in an era that is post-truth means we live in an era with other things, namely emotions and preferences dictate arguments and decision-making. Opinions and convictions are now being formed based on attachments unrelated to the truth of a person or their concepts. One nice consequence of naming "post-truth" is that the term passively recognizes that truth is something that once existed, or may even exist still under the rubble and stains of so much narcissism. So what is a follower of St. Nicholas to do?

The process starts with asking critical questions. I don't mean to be critical of others personally or to appear cynical on all fronts. Simply put, things cannot be accepted on face value in any culture and we need to be able to dig deeper. Convictions and opinions need to be explored. More questions need to be asked. We live in an era where so many of our leaders and so much of mass marketing is treating us, intentionally – like stupid sheep. Don't run with the masses. Even in the busyness and hectic nature of our lives – we need to lift our heads from time to time and ask some critical questions. Increasingly, young people and their friends will present arguments and positions that are disconnecting from logic and reality and they'll do so with passionate confidence. Recall, several generations have been shaped by the idea that they have a universal right to no universal truth – but instead a unilateral right towards the world conforming to whatever ideas they espouse. This modern reality and its atmosphere requires vigilance and patience. While it's doubtful that someone will declare a catholic global conference on universal truth and relativism, a remnant portion of people must remain committed to questioning the deeper "post-truth" realities that exist. In this spirit, as followers of St. Nicholas, we must fight being compliant with the philosophical direction of the modern western world. It's unlikely that we'll need to take to the streets or form ecumenical councils to move forward, but instead, we must be willing to take a stand and at least question the direction of the herd.

Simultaneously, we live in an era with a cacophony of false teachings. These teachings cross old lines of Catholic-Protestant or Lutheran – Calvin. In a "post-truth" world, relativism and the wholesale rejection of authority has empowered people to create new concepts regarding words like "tolerance", "marriage", "love", "life" and "acceptance". Not only are words and their meanings being disconnected from previous understood realities, but new meanings are being attached to words like "bigot" and "close-minded" and "hateful". Difficult and worthwhile conversations and explorations about truly valid questions and interpretations are set aside for hashtags and insta-posts. Reactions and outbursts are lifted-up while thoughtful dialogues and friendships are muted. Within this fractured and disintegrating landscape, followers of St Nicholas must find a way to maintain friendships while asking simple questions. There is a manner in which a person needs to engage this arena – gentleness, humility and conviction.

But there's more – St Nicholas didn't just engage the largest question of the day at the Council of Nicaea, but he also took on the largest dynamic in the world of worship – the system of pagan idol temple worship. For centuries, the Roman state system of religion relied on a connection between the worship of pagan gods (usually stemming from the Greek system of gods) and the worship of the Roman State and its Emperor. While it's hard for Americans to fathom, the worship of pagan gods and the Emperor was not simply a once-a-week act, but was embedded in the culture through rituals, economies and festivals. Whole cities and marketplaces were established around the worship of gods and the Emperor that led to ancillary issues like temple prostitution and consecrated food. In a simple sense, this system of worship was the combination of the local strip mall, the houses of worship and federal government; all in one convenient avenue, complete with a calendar of festivals and obligations. The beauty of the system is that it gave room for personal preference and need – you could worship Zeus or Apollo depending on the situation. If you were going to be a participating person or family in the lifeblood of the Roman Empire, you had to worship idols and your Emperor. The worship life of Romans and the 4th Century was a virtual cornucopia of options and flavors.

Against this backdrop, both Jews and Christians marched in a different direction. They taught that that worshipping anyone but God (Yahweh or Jesus) was forbidden. Imagine the shock for a person considering Christianity when they learned that they would need to stop celebrating at festivals or making offerings at a favorite temple or even eating the roasted lamb sold out of the basement of a favorite worship site. Leaving behind a worship life of a Roman polis would have been a heavy consideration – the social loss alone would have been immense. And still, against all these odds and costs, the Christian movement in the Roman Empire grew.

As Constantine developed his rule as Emperor, he first loosened the laws against Christian worship and the persecution of Christians. He secondly began to allow the cleaning out of Roman temples provided the statuary and valuable art works be deposited in the royal treasury (he was a frugal reformer).

Once again, St Nicholas lived in a transitional time. Within his Diocese (the geographic area where he had spiritual authority), the worship of the Goddess of Artemis was particularly widespread. Artemis was a daughter of Zeus and twin-sister to Apollo. She was connected to women in particular, specializing in fertility and virginity. She was a strong goddess and was most often portrayed with a bow for the hunt. Her statue with her stag in hand in the galleries of the Louvre in Paris today still stuns visitors who pass by her way. The Greeks and Romans loved her so much that her Temple in Ephesus was considered one of the 7 wonders of the ancient world – on par with the Pyramids in Egypt. Artemis worship had two festivals and her temples were widespread throughout the region where St Nicholas walked. We can imagine the primary and secondary worship practices surrounding a goddess who's focus was fertility and virginity. It's staggering to consider what licenses must have been given freely in the ancient Roman world under the meaning of "worship" in the name of Artemis.

As Constantine began to transition the Empire from pagan worship to Christian worship, the allowance for the cleaning out of pagan temples meant turning the social, economic and spiritual lives of entire cities upside down. St Nicholas was up to the task. Stories of are told of Nicholas moving from town to town, village to village, city to city, preaching about Christ and His worship and exhorting people to leave idol worship and Artemis behind. Several ancient biographers of Nicholas tell about his zealous and passionate pleas to leave their pagan worship and come to the worshipping life of the ancient church. And so we see in Nicholas a person who was not only dedicated to the Truth in hallways of an ecumenical council regarding the highest truths of God and His being, but also a person who preached the truth in squares and marketplaces, begging and inviting people to leave behind the meaninglessness of their idol worship.

What is our marketplace of worship today?

While we may sense a detachment from the houses of worship, the marketplace and the worship of the State – surely these circles intersect even for the modern person. At its basest form, worship is the act of giving sacrifice to that "thing" that you treat as holy or "other" than you. Seen in this sense – more people in the west worship money than any other deity. Rather than give all to God – we give what's left over to Him and spend our lives worshipping (giving) to the system that promises comfort, prosperity and health. In many ways, we're not any more sophisticated today than the Romans were 1700 years ago. We have our festivals and rituals attached to our consumerism or workaholic lifestyles. We offer sincere and whole sacrifices of our lives and money to economic systems and promises – consider how many young people today are signing up for a lifetime of crippling debt just for the privilege of the "college experience" and the promise that a degree will lend itself to security. Where the Romans sacrificed a lamb or a bull for health or good fortune, we willingly sacrifice our time, energy and resources to the college, the employer or even a product out of the same hope.

If Nicholas preached in the marketplaces against the worship of pagan gods and invited people into the worship of Christ – what would he preach today? Ironically – if they gave the mic to Santa Claus at the end of the Macy's Day Parade – what would his message be? Would we expect the Saint to preach conformity to an economic system of worship that asks you for everything, promises you everything and delivers almost nothing? Or would he plead with you and I to find our meaning and our purpose and our sacrifice in the worship life of Christ and his Church?

In my own life as a Catholic Deacon and youth minister, I've had the opportunity to live in the marketplace and the sanctuary. As the Saint was wooing me to his way of life, I had one encounter that stands out to me in particular. We were over in small village in Poland in preparation for the World Youth Days in 2016. We were working with a local priest and the parishes in town and by serving through small acts of charity and service in the day and having fun, energetic meetings at night. Each night I was called forth to share the Gospel and the simple truth of God's love for each of us. Over the course of the week, the crowd grew from 200 to roughly 600 by the end of the week. We had to move the gatherings from a classroom to the town municipal meeting space. One of the coordinators of the week was a woman named Tyna from the Czech Republic who is easily on her pathway to sainthood.

We had our picture taken together after one of the liturgies – while I still in my alb and stole. As she was scrolling through the pictures on her phone with a young Polish leader, the young woman stopped her and said, "Go back to that picture of you with the Saint." Tyna inquired about which picture and the young woman said, "The one with you and St. Nicholas." She scrolled back to the one of me and her and exclaimed, "That one! That's the picture!" Tyna asked her, "You mean the one with me and the Deacon?" And the young girl said – "That's the face of St. Nicholas because he always shared the truth." Obviously, when Tyna relayed that story to me I was stunned. But then, each night as I would walk with the crowd to the meeting space, this young Polish college girl would come up alongside of me with a huge grin and sing, "You better watch out, you better not hide, you better not pout I'm telling you why, Santa Claus is coming to town" and then flit away into the crowd. Obviously my head began to spin, but one of the convictions that took a deeper root in my life that week was the necessity to stand up for the truth and declare that truth with boldness, humility and invitation.

We began this Rule considering generosity. Generosity as a lifestyle directed against the materialism of today. Generosity as an escape opportunity against so many of contemporary pressures and values. Our second Rule gave us a direction for that generosity – in spirit and practice. Children, their safety and development, provide a pure conduit for us to direct our attention and resources. And here, in the Third Rule, we find that Standing for the Truth invites us not only to question the direction of the modern world and the "lostness" of its very foundations, but a deeper opportunity to zealously invite others into another way to live. What if someone appeared in your neighborhood that was kind, gentle, humble, generous and cared for children in a unique and special way? What if that person by virtue of their lifestyle and words began to invite you to work less, acquire less, give more, laugh more, take more time off and to clear your calendar for times of personal devotion and the age-old practice of Sunday liturgy? Wouldn't that person be like a Saint to you? Wouldn't that person be like St. Nicholas to you?

Now – what if that person was you?

The Fourth Rule

Work for Justice

St Nicholas worked for justice.

There may seem like a contradiction that the patron saint of
children is also the patron saint of prisoners. To start, Bishop
Nicholas was most likely prisoned in his home province during
the great persecution under Emperor Diocletia before
Constantine's reign began and the Bishops were released. In
fact, rumors of Nicholas' torture have some modern
circumstantial validation. When Nicholas's bones were removed
and studied in 2004, his skull was digitally recreated using
contemporary technology. The doctors concluded that Nicholas'
nose had been broken – and historians began to wonder if this
came during his imprisonment or during that speculative brawl at
the Council of Nicaea. The consideration that Santa Claus
spent significant time in a Roman jail and perhaps suffered under
torturous conditions is a wonderous contradiction. Imagining our
Saint strolling the dark streets and tossing bags of coins into
windows or reuniting slave kids to their parents fits well.
Picturing Nicholas chained to a wall and having his face
punched in gives us a more challenging and difficult reality.

Of course, the stories don't stop with his imprisonment.

There is another story of three young soldiers or sailors who
were wrongly accused of a capital crime. The dispute took place
in Andriaki, the local port near Nicholas' home. Bishop
Nicholas was already in the area, helping to put down the drama
when word came that these three young men were about to be
put to death. Nicholas arrived on the scene quickly and stopped

the executioner's sword as he looked to separate the men's heads from their bodies. Not only were the young men spared, but Nicholas took the extra measure to ensure that the men's names were cleared of any wrongdoing.

In Nicholas' actions we see the super-hero image being born again. Quick to action – quick to right a wrong; Nicholas knew what it was like to suffer for being wrongly accused because he had paid his own personal cost before. And so with Saint Nicholas we see a different type of justice-maker – he's an active participant. As we saw before, he didn't lack for intellect or depth, and we don't have reports that he was impertinent or impatient – but we get the strong impression that St. Nicholas was not the type to form a committee or wait for a review to come in. Where there were unjust situations, he took actions. This reality is a familiar thread through all the stories. Bags of gold, swords being stopped, kids in pickle barrels – where there is wrong, it is corrected.

We might be looking for some wriggle room here to we can duck this type of responsibility, but there's still more. The story goes that Nicholas' region was suffering a severe famine. During the period, a large shipment of wheat was headed out of region to the port of Alexandria. Rather than sit back, Nicholas headed to the port and worked to negotiate some grain for the people. The merchants refused saying that the shipment had already been precisely measured out. Being Saint Nicholas, he assured the men that if they would measure out grain from each ship for the people, when they arrived in Alexandra, their shipment would miraculously remain full. He succeeded in persuading the merchants towards his position and the grain was put to quick use to bring relief to the people. Likewise,

Nicholas (or God) held up the other end of the bargain and the full shipment arrived in the Port of Alexandria as agreed upon.

The issue for us here is that if Nicholas' pursuit of justice-creating actions were limited to life-and-death issues or concerns of jail and prison, we could easily claim that we lack the power to help, unless you're a lawyer or a judge or a legislator. But this other story surrounding the wheat and the famine expands the need to act justly beyond the courtroom and speaks of basic humans rights and needs. No one is disqualified from creating a more just world where people have what they need in the most basic sense. Notice again, Nicholas' brand of justice is centered around action. In the story of the three innocents, he simply intervened. In the story with merchants and the famine, he intervened but it involved faith. Active faith = he made a promise on the premise that God would honor the bargain because to do so was fully consistent with the character of God.

This merging of faith and action speaks to the center of spirituality in the vein of St Nicholas. To follow the Saint, we must be active — but it's not action for the sake of movement. The actions we take are rooted in faith-filled anticipation of God making the future of the world, the city, the neighborhood, the parish, the family or the child better. There is an under-girding confidence that "if we leap, He will catch us." The action is random and its never self-seeking. We push our limits and we are open to make mistakes as we seek solutions to problems, small and large.

I've been brought to the edge of these moments many times.

In my role as a Deacon and youth minister, I've been blessed to build a relationship with a series of villages in a region of rural

El Salvador. For well over a decade, my friends and I have been privileged to bring young American teenagers and some adults to these villages to build friendships, do projects, bring medical care and celebrate God's goodness. The fruit of these relationships has been beyond life-changing and the whole experience is well beyond my grasp. Our friends in rural El Salvador are among the "poorest of the poor" and yet, they have schooled us all in hospitality, generosity, faithfulness and joy. I am humbled and proud to call the village of Rancho Grande a second home.

And here's where Saint Nicholas comes in.

Like the envelopes of cash that started to show up on the porch, resources for our friends in El Salvador pour in and through our hands. We are a non-profit and our promise to our friends has simply been – "whatever God gives us, we'll give to you." It turns out that God really loves our friends because I've never witnessed such a consistent and steady stream of resources. From one unlikely source (Upstate NY teenagers) to an unknown recipient (rural El Salvadoran farmers), every year – more and more funds and resources come in and larger and greater projects get accomplished.

About midway through the development of this relationship, I was growing frustrated with my ability to execute projects in the rural countryside. Oftentimes, we were flush with cash and we would have 100· American teenagers ready to work, but we were working in an environment were supplies came late (if at all), contractors were few, tools couldn't be found and schedules couldn't be kept. Progress would always be made and the people were amazing; it just became heartbreaking that so many of the easy things we take for granted in America were so hard there.

One particular year, things were going slowly and we didn't have the tools we needed to utilize all the kids we had. I had money for tools, but no access to them. Out of frustration, I took the rental pick-up truck and decided to go for a ride – not the usually recommended response for a person in rural El Salvador but I needed to pray. I drove back through the dirt fields and the tiny villages and made my way to the Texaco to fill the truck with gas. I had made this right hand turn off the main drag at the Texaco for years – it was a unchanging landmark for directions and this Texaco sort of demarked entry into this land of extreme poverty.

After filling up the truck with gas, I parked the truck in a parking spot and prayed. I remembered St. Nicholas and I prayed to him – I asked him for help. I was frustrated. Here we were with cash and kids for labor and no tools. I poured out my heart to St Nicholas asking him for relief and help.

As I lifted up my eyes to the rearview mirror, something caught my eye. A huge sign hung above the business across the street – San Nicolas Ferreteria y Materials. I had driven on this road dozens – if not a hundred times. My view had always been to turn right at the Texaco gas station – everything about my direction and my attention was to the villages we were going to. Everything was about the destination and arriving there. I had never noticed that there was a St. Nicholas Hardware & Materials store across the street!!

I was overjoyed – and laughing. I pulled over and bought dozens of pickaxes and shovels and crow bars and bounded back to Rancho Grande and our kids got right to work. As I asked the villagers about it – they told me that the name of the town north of them, along the main drag was called San Nicholas. I had been coming to rural El Salvador for years and was growing in my awareness and devotion to St. Nicholas and never once knew that we all drove through his town to get to our friends. I had to chuckle – he had outfoxed me again. Here I thought I was doing something – active faith – out of devotion to his way of living and he had a whole town there decades before.

San Nicholas Hardware and Materials Store.

That storefront fits for St. Nicholas style of justice. At a base level, justice is the righting of wrongs, the fixing of broken things, the correcting of mistaken ways. Justice has the element of restoration to it – the making of things the way they were intended. It was intended that everyone should be able to eat and live without hunger they didn't chose. It is intended that innocent people should not pay for crimes. Justice demands that kidnapped children be returned to their parents. Oftentimes we see justice on the opposite side of the scale from proclamation or evangelism. Rarely do we see the evangelical partnering passionately with the social justice warrior and vice versa. A false and unnecessary chasm has existed that puts people into camps – people say things like, "what the point of feeding them if they don't know Jesus or the Gospel?" and others say things like, "if you're not willing to feed them, why tell that God loves them?" The figure of St. Nicholas destroys that barrier and grabs both camps and demands action in the present tense.

Actions for justice in the present tense. As we saw in the Third Rule, St Nicholas does not shy away from proclaiming and standing for the truth – but as we're seeing here – he's not simply a preacher or teacher, but also is someone that is passionately active and concerned about justice for his people. In the life of Nicholas, we see the embodiment of both virtues. The most relevant icons of Saint Nicholas show him holding the Bible – this points to his passion as a preacher and teacher and his dedication to the truth against false teachings and idols. But then all the stories of Nicholas show the justice side – restoring families, saving kids, providing grain, stopping unjust punishments. In Nicholas spirituality, there's no room for a one-sided approach.

Another way to see Nicholas' sense of present-moment active justice is through the corporal acts of mercy.

The Seven Corporal Acts of Mercy are plain:

Feed the Hungry
Give Drink to the Thirsty
Shelter the Homeless
Visit the Sick
Visit the Prisoners
Bury the Dead
Give alms to the Poor

The simple power of these seven actions and encouragements is that they are written in the present tense and they can be done today. Maybe you're not in position to bury the dead today, but you can always give to the poor or help to feed the hungry. Every city in the country has a homeless shelter and nearly every town and village has a food pantry. Nearly all of these are run by people of faith and the need for volunteers is extraordinary. In most instances, others have done the work to provide the venue of our service. We simply need to show up.

This vision for justice and active mercy affects our generosity as well. We talked early about directing our resources to children and causes and venues where they are protected and nourished. Nicholas' spirit of justice challenges outside of those arenas into areas of prison ministries and homeless shelters and hospital chaplaincy. Where we are unable to physically help those in need, others can do it and very often, they need our financial support to maintain and expand their care.

We're not burdened to have to say yes to every financial need of every agency, but as followers of Nicholas, we are called to have faith that as we're generous and spread our the good seed as far and as wide as we can, our resources will be replenished.

Perhaps another word describes St. Nicholas justice as well. —

"Go"

This word challenges our new, contemporary false definition of action. On Twitter and Instagram, we "follow" people. People ask — "how many followers do you have?" But when Jesus invited — "Come follow me..." the intention was that people would go somewhere. Literally — they would "pick up their nets and leave the boat behind." Active justice does not "go" by checking a box or clicking to give $5 to a cause after a hurricane. St. Nicholas justice "goes" — it is present — it shows up.

I have a friend in my city who is a widow. Her priest is a great guy and their parish was on the edge of some real poverty and homelessness. She was a retired nurse and he approached her to start up something to help the people. They started with sandwiches. They'd drive around at night and find people —

everywhere: corners, parks, under bridges... and they'd drop off their sandwiches and make a friendship. Before long they needed a van and the runs got longer and more involved. They decided they were starting a ministry and they named it "Emmaus Ministry" because the story of the Emmaus walk on Easter Sunday is that Jesus walked alongside the two weary travelers as they made their way home. Over a very short time, my friend brought some of her nursing background and her organizational skills to bear and a building was rented right in the heart of the crisis of poverty. These are some of the toughest and most desperate streets in our country and my friend just settled in. Not long into that project, another building became available for expansion and what was once two people serving sandwiches out of a van has exploded into a stunning operation that touches hundreds of people and stands as a beacon of light in the darkness and hope where despair has reigned.

What was the secret to my friends' success and fruit? They went. They took action. They didn't have in mind the wonderous things God has done and I don't think they even know what He'll do next — but where they saw a need and they had ability and resources — they took action. They didn't take action by researching and complaining or forming a committee or taking a poll. They made some sandwiches and started to hand them out to hungry people.

It was that way for us in El Salvador. On our first trip there, we had a pediatrician with us in order to keep our own kids safe and sound. By the end of the trip, some villagers had learned of his training and asked if he would look at a baby. We sat on the back of a pick-up truck our my friend gave his first examination. He then saw some other kids and to be honest — they didn't look so good. I asked him what was the issue and he had me listen to the belly of one of the youngsters. He was about 5 years old and had a big round belly. When I put the scope in my ears, I could hear things moving – but didn't understand what it was. My doctor friend told me that the sound was worms. He told me that there was nothing to be done for these kids and people until they had access to clean water.

That's where St. Nicholas justice comes in.

I'm not a doctor and I'm not an engineer, but I know people. I got some friends together and we came back to the village 5 months later. I told some high school kids to find out who we needed to talk to in El Salvador about putting a well in that village and within two weeks I had received an email from the head of a clean water organization. A month before we returned the following year, I received pictures in my email from two wells being drilled well beyond the depth where safe water lies. Clean water had come to Rancho Grande. Since that first bold action of simply providing clean access to clean water for 45 families, the movement for clean water in the region has exploded. Both Rancho Grande and its neighboring village have their own municipal water system that provides clean water 24 hours a day, 7 days a week. How hundreds of families have access to clean drinking water in their homes and the village is growing! This would have been beyond imagination for anyone the first day we showed up and looked at those kids on the back of that pickup truck. Beyond that, clean water is produced and delivered to hundreds of other families and other villages have received their own clean water systems that fit the local issues they struggle with.

We had no intention of bringing clean water to thousands of people when we sat on the truck – but we did have a simple premise at the center of our activity – Go. The first step was a well. There was simply nothing else to do. For my friends on the southside, the first act of creating present-tense justice was sandwiches. You may feel your action or contribution is small – its not. What's the difference you can make today – where you are and with what you have? What is the wrong that can be corrected or the restoration that can be created?

Now St. Nicholas was a Bishop – because of that title, he started his "career" in jail. But later, that position gave him influence and authority. He used the position to serve. What's your position? Seen this way, it doesn't matter if you're a shop clerk at the local grocery store or the CEO of the whole chain – what's your position? Are you in charge of bringing justice through action to the person in your check-out line? Or are you in charge of bringing restoration to 1000 employees? The myth would be that either my role is too small to matter or too big to make any changes. In reality, neither is more "important" than the other – what matters is that we use our positions in life to bring justice on earth in the present tense.

Seen in this light, the spirit and activity of St. Nicholas justice answers a critical component of our Lord's prayer: "Thy Kingdom come, thy will be done on earth as it is in Heaven."

This is a present-tense prayer. Though Heaven is a future-tense place for us, it is also present-tense reality in the prayer. Heaven is many things and among them, it is place of ultimate justice and restoration. St Nicholas lived his life in that present-tense moment and then his works continued well beyond the grave. The veil between Heaven and earth was lifted through his episcopal ministry, including his active work of justice.

'What are you waiting for? 'What can you do today for to bring justice and God's Kingdom to earth'?

The Fifth Rule

Live with Joy

Associating joy with St. Nicholas isn't too much of a stretch. Remember – he's a right "jolly ole jolly ole elf" right? But where does that joy and that power find its source?

After Bishop Nicholas died, he was buried in a crypt in Myra, his home town and the center of his diocese and ministry. Over the centuries, people would make a pilgrimage to his grave just to venerate the Saint. Oftentimes, the story went that the crypt had a sweet aroma and there was a mysterious liquid ooze coming from the tomb itself.

Over 600 years after his death, Christians from mainland Europe became concerned because of the stories of marauding Muslim crusaders from the Middle East that were making their way through modern-day Turkey and desecrating Christian Holy sites. Some particularly prickly Crusaders from Italy decided to head over to Myra, snatch up Nicholas' bones and transport them safely back to a more protected country.

The heist wasn't without issue, but in the end, Nicholas – bones and all came by boat to the port town of Bari, Italy. The date of their arrival was May 9th, 1087. The townspeople quickly got to work and built a Basilica his honor complete with an underground crypt just for St. Nicholas. In 1089, Pope Urban II came and moved the holy man's bones into their final resting place. That date survives to this day as the centerpiece of an enormous three-day festival in Bari all they way to modern day.

We have to pause and recall just how ancient St. Nicholas was. He was known as a "wonderworker" well beyond his death and the average person's devotion to him was so significant over 600 years after his death that not only was an effort made to save and move his bones — but a celebration broke out around their safe keeping that has been continuous for over 1000 years. Can we think of anyone that even comes close to that kind of revelry around their bones?

Once placed in his final sarcophocos, the bones began to do their mysterious work. As they had in Myra, they began to ooze a myrrh-like substance. This liquid began to be collected annually by the local Bishop and cut together with Holy Water and distributed throughout the region for the healing of illnesses. This practice continues to this day and of course the day that they collect the "manna" is May 9th.

The bones themselves were first studied in 1954 when the tomb needed restoration. They were found to be the skeleton of a slight man who died in his 70s — matching the historical story of St. Nicholas the person. But to the surprise of everyone, while the bones were out of the grave and in the lab, the very linen sheet that held them seemed to develop a layer of moisture on top!

We had heard about Bari and researched about the bones and the myrrh. For our 20th anniversary, we saved up some money and decided to do a once-in-a-lifetime trip to Rome and Bari. We wined and dined and saw incredible things in Rome and then took the train over to Bari on the east coast as a pilgrimage. Now at this point, my wife was suffering from extreme lactose intolerance. We had learned that generally, food in Europe was more acceptable to her system. It was a condition that had really developed after her second pregnancy and had become so extreme that it was really interfering with her enjoyment of any food or any social event that surrounded food.

We settled into our apartment and spent the first day and evening getting familiar with the Old Town of Bari – a beautiful maze of limestone housing built straight up off of centuries old stone pathways. After enjoying an expresso and pastry in the square next to the Basilica the next morning, we ventured into the sacred space. The sanctuary on the main floor is wonderful – lighthearted – ancient and grand. There is a different feel than what we had experienced in the grandeur of Rome – a lighter touch and a simpler tone.

As we walked slowly about the sanctuary, we noticed that the steps down to the tomb were towards the front, on either side. We entered expectantly from the left side.

What we encountered was beyond our belief.

We entered into a bright space filled with aromatic sensations. As we crossed the threshold, our ears were overwhelmed with the rich and deep baritone sounds of Russian Orthodox priests leading a group of women pilgrims in prayer. Their heads covered, they sang the choruses while the priests led the stanzas. We slowly walked deeper into the space. There were pews with seating for up to 400 (my guess) people and special paintings and sculptures throughout. At the front and center was an altar with a hole in the floor beneath it – this was all protected by a cage but it was evident that Nicholas was below the altar.

We took a seat in the third pew and began to take it all in. Where I expected a dark and perhaps dingy 1000 year-old crypt, we encountered a rich and vibrant worship space unlike anything we had ever experienced. We prayed the Liturgy of the Hours and continued to soak in the experience. Scores and scores of pilgrims came in – praying at the altar with sincerity and passion and moving slowly through the space. Tourists came too and they lingered, perhaps less comfortable but struck by the wonder of the atmosphere.

More than an hour passed. We were at complete peace. Finally, I said to my wife, "Get up, let's go." We left our belongings in the pew and I brought her up to Nicholas. We knelt as close as we could to the altar and placed my hands on her belly. I prayed as hard as I knew how to – prayed that God would heal my wife's stomach and this terrible disorder that made her life so tough.

As we knelt and prayed, a handful of women with scarves over their heads got behind us and joined us in our prayer. I realized that they must have thought that my wife was barren the way I was laying my hands on her belly. We kept praying. I don't know how long we were up there, but I prayed as passionately as I knew how to. After a period of time, we returned to the pews and just continued to soak up the atmosphere.

We were in a crypt – of a person who was buried there over a thousand years ago – who lived over 1600 years from that moment. And yet there was a personality, a warmth, a presence that was thick. When we think of Santa Claus, there are words that come to mind: friendliness, caring, merry, giving, generous, happy – simply put – JOY. How was it possible that we could be sitting in the space of an ancient dead man and be experiencing a physical feeling of joy? Over the coming hour or so, roughly two to three hundred more people passed through. These were mostly pilgrims but we were stunned. While we were down there, perhaps as many as 500 people came through, and this was just a day in the middle of October.

I've visited graves before. I remember being struck by the humility and the simplicity of George and Martha Washington's graves at Mt. Vernon. For such a historical giant of man to be buried so simply and in such a beautiful setting was a statement of humility and service. I remember being at Mao's Tomb in Beijing. To stand in line with hundreds of Chinese people, forced to buy a carnation and bow in worship before an orange-faced leader, frozen in a plastic chamber, guarded by stiff-faced soldiers was harrowing. The tomb itself is dropped in the middle of Tienamann's square as an epic reminder to the people that the Party interrupts the imperial flow from the Temple to the Forbidden City. Where Washington's grave preached humility, Mao's screamed power and dominance.

But Nicholas's grave – this space exuded joy. A physical experience, a marinade in a personality. Healing, worship, gratitude, happiness, light.

We gathered ourselves and went back into the square. They were preparing for a wedding and an enormous white runner was being managed and unrolled down the main center aisle. We headed left to the gift shop and looked at the icons. From behind the counter, we spotted the myrrh for sale and bought several vials of both the water and the oil versions. We didn't know what had happened with Tammy's belly yet, but we weren't going to pass up the opportunity to bless others with what we had experienced.

We left Bari and returned home a few days later. We were excited to see if the Saint had healed her disorder and so we went out for a rich and full Italian meal. We ordered cheesy garlic bread and red wine. After that, we asked for fettuccini alfredo just to really push the envelope. The very mention of those meals before – or their appearance at a table close by was enough to turn my wife's stomach into a 6-month pregnant bloat. And here we are, just about a week after returning from Nicholas's tomb – testing the waters.

As we enjoyed the bread, the wine and the pasta, my wife began to smile, and to cry and then to laugh. There was no bloating, there was no pain, there was no discomfort. Years have passed since that afternoon in Bari and to this day, my wife can eat and drink whatever she wants with no affects. We had lived with the terrible debilitation of extreme lactose intolerance and St. Nicholas and his healing prayers set her free.

As the story of Tammy's healing spread, we gained the opportunity to bless people with the Saint's myrrh. Without going into details about other people's healings, we haven't been disappointed. Sometimes people are a little uneasy since they may not understand the idea of invoking the prayers of a Saint, but we reassure them and simply pray for their intercession while blessing them with the myrrh. Time and time again, people have found their bodies coming back to normal – sometimes quickly and sometimes over time. In some instances, things previously undiagnosed have been able to be figured out by physicians previously confused by symptoms. There is no particular way that the healings have come and not all of them have been total, but no one has been disappointed by the outcomes.

A year or two later, my wife suffered a terrible injury to her foot — something called a Lisfranc partial tear. In essence, through a freak accident, the tiny rubber-band ligament that rests on top of the bones of her foot suffered a tear. The injury is incredibly painful and takes roughly a year to heal if surgery can be avoided.

Trusting the doctors we endured the year of being in a boot, hobbling, crutches, pain, "two steps forward one step back" type stuff. Over the course of the year, I would bless her foot with one of the vials of St Nicholas' myrrh. Especially when the pain would increase, I would gently rub the myrrh on her foot and pray for God to bring her relief and healing. I must have done this 50-60 times throughout the year.

About halfway through the year, I realized something strange was happening with the vial of myrrh. I had been blessing my wife for months with the stuff and the vial was still full. Truthfully, I never poured it out or anything, but I would pour it on my fingers and then caress her foot with the liquid. After a full year of blessing her, that vial rested on top of my dresser without a drop missing.

Over time, her foot did heal and she returned pretty much to her normal routine but the comfort brought by the prayers and blessings with the myrrh where central to her faith in the healing process.

Our trip to the Nicholas' crypt prepared us for an even more critical moment. Within 3 weeks of returning from Bari, I learned from a urologist that I had life-threatening scores related to prostate cancer. Being younger than most men who receive a prostate cancer diagnosis, I was at even greater risk. We had to act quickly and surgery was scheduled that winter. I had never imagined facing a cancer diagnosis – no one in my entire extended family had experienced cancer. Likewise, we had no expectation of facing something mortal in nature. In a very short season, we had to make some big decisions about how we were going to endure this tribulation.

My thoughts returned to Nicholas's tomb. Joy. The author of Hebrews tells us that is was "for joys sake that Jesus endured the cross, scorning its shame." St James tells us similarly to "consider it pure joy when you face trials of all kinds" Taken together, facing the cancer, the implications of the surgery physically, the road to recovery and so much that was out of our hands, we could chose joy.

Nicholas was dead and yet his grave literally oozed joy. Here was our moment. It turns out that the healing from lactose intolerance was just a sign, a bread crumb; the deeper healing came later. Faced with the opportunity to worry, despair and sink into depression, my spirit was buoyed and strengthened with joy. The surgery itself and the ins-and-outs of recovery were opportunities for negativity and fear – or joy and hope.

In the months around my surgery and recovery, there were physical moments that were difficult and trying. At the same time, our family laughed and celebrated as much as ever before. Perhaps as important, my wife and boys were watching me. Fear has a way of spreading. Anxiety creeps in and plants terrible seeds in our minds and hearts. Joy and hope work in powerful ways too – replenishing our soil with goodness and opening our minds to great possibilities.

Consider what our world needs today: fear and anxiety or joy and hope? Which forces are more powerful? Our world's natural default is to promote the negative – we need to be purposeful and intentional about fostering the positive.

Joy is the anecdote to a world living in hysterical anxiety. Joy is the healing companion through trials and darkness. Joy is the ingredient that allows for new possibilities to emerge from previously "dead" outcomes.

On Christmas Eve, the angel declares to the shepherds, "Fear not, for behold, I bring you tidings of great joy that shall be for all the people." Joy announces good things. Joy creates new spaces. And joy is a choice.

Joy is not like happiness or foolishness. Joy is a calculated decision to believe in something that has yet to happen – to see something that is possible – to chose to laugh in pain and draw from deep within to anticipate good things. Joy is not married to outcomes and doesn't expect immediate results. Joy can not be taken away easily for it has the power to build upon itself. The contagious nature of joy is mirrored by the way that light cannot be held by darkness.

And does this not bring us to the figure of Santa Claus?

Much has been studied and made of the long transformation from the Bishop of Myra to the Santa Claus of the West. The story is an incredible journey through history. From the moment the Puritans and the settlers of Jamestown settled in colonial America and even all the way into the beginning of the modern era, celebrations of holidays were a contentious topic. Far ranging and hard-formed opinions reigned. The Puritans forbad the celebration of Christmas and certainly any praying or associations with a Saint figure. Things weren't much different for most Protestants who were very nervous and prickly about any possible false worship of idols and revelry that might distract from pure worship.

Against that backdrop, Nicholas was brought to the "New World" by Dutch sailors and bankers who kept a low-profile through modern-day Manhattan and Pennsylvania. After the miraculous victory for Independence, New Yorkers began to embrace their Dutch roots with more pride and when they formed the New York Historical Society in 1804, they chose Nicholas as the Patron Saint for both the Society and the city. As their operations began to ramp up, influential member Washington Irving wrote a fictional history of New York in 1809 which featured a jolly St. Nicholas figure. This figure wasn't the Saint from Myra, but instead a Dutch burglar who snuck into homes to deliver presents to children; an elfish figure complete with a clay pipe. The work was a hit and historians credit Irving with penning the first American work of *imagination*.

We can see how Irving's adaptation of St. Nicholas would later influence the author of "Twas the Night Before Christmas (or A Visit from St. Nicholas." While the authorship is disputed, by 1824, the vision of St Nicholas jumping from rooftop to rooftop and scaling chimneys with a bag of gifts was cemented.

But perhaps more important than the transformation is the word *imagination*. We could do a deep-dive into the importance of imagination at the center of the American psyche and posture. As we consider living a life of joy, imagination becomes a necessary companion. Without imagination, a person can't see reality beyond its current constraints. Without imagination, circumstances begin to weigh beyond possibilities, In an experience without imagination, there is little hope, creativity is cut-off and openness to the unknown, even God is marginal. Is it possible that the figure of Santa Claus has stuck around with such vigor in the American mindset because we long for and need a home for our imaginative and joyful thoughts?

Ask any kid – who's more reliable and joyful than St. Nicholas?

But of course, as with everything St. Nicholas, legend meets history. In 1916, Greek immigrants began Orthodox worship services in a tavern down on the tip of Manhattan. After several years, five families bought the building and began to build a church on the site. They dedicated the church to St. Nicholas and the congregation began to grow. Of course, Manhattan began to grow as well and the by the end of the century, a little church dedicated to St. Nicholas sat directly under the enormous bulk of the south tower of the World Trade Center.

On September 11th, 2001 that same South Tower fell directly onto St. Nicholas Church. The heart of the City fell onto the home of the City's Saint. While the entire World Center Complex continues to be rebuilt, so is the church. As it nears completion, space has been dedicated on the second floor for people of all faiths to come and reflect, pray and mediate. A space to take a break from the pace, pressure and strain of working in New York City's financial district. Officials estimate once St. Nicholas' church and national shrine open, it will be the most visited church in America.

And so we have to wonder – how does the man who died in Myra in the 4th century end up with his bones buried on the western coast of the Adriatic after 600 years and then with a church in the most influential city in the world that will attract the most visitors that will be dedicated to him 1700 years after his death?

It goes further – Nicholas II, the last tsar of Russia had gifted relics of St. Nicholas to that little church in Manhattan. Those sacred pieces – ties to the original Saint were lost to the ground on 9/11. Think of this- along with the over 3,000 souls lost to eternity and the horrifying loss of human life and flesh – amidst that global and calamitous tragedy are buried physical connections to Saint Nicholas, the patron saint of New York.

There are churches dedicated to St. Nicholas all over the country. What are the odds? What are the chances that our very own St. Nicholas and his relics would be lost to the world on 9/11? What are the chances that 1700 year old relics would be buried forever with the victims of the attack in the same city that he presides over? New York City alone is a huge city with thousands of churches? What are the odds that the church destroyed on that terrible day is Nicholas's church?

It's enough to make you smile. When that Bishop started chucking gold bags through windows to save young girls, what measure of imagination would it have taken to even conceive that one day in the impossible-to-see future – that same man would be physically connected to a City in a far-off land with the victims of an attack from a inconceivable source? With the stories of St. Nicholas we enter into a space that goes beyond imagination. We are entering into the space of incarnation. And even better – of resurrection.

Without imagination, what do we have? Can we really conceive of the Immaculate Conception, the Virgin birth and the Feeding of the 5,000 without some imagination? As we march towards our own mortality – can we ourselves imagine a personal eternal home with love and worship without a measure of imagination?

The cross does not take imagination. Pain, suffering, torture, abuse – these are hard-learned realities that are in union with and universal to the human condition.

But faith, hope, love – eternal life and victory over death – these take other means. Joy and its happy companion imagination take us to the places of possibility, change, transformation and resurrection. Google is great if you want information, or even misinformation – but totally useless if you want imagination.

One of St. Nicholas' nicknames is "Wonderworker". This tag comes from all the works he's done since he's been dead over 1600 years ago. I don't think the Christmas presents are a even a consideration here – but if you piled that on to all the miracles (and the kids think they should be added)- can you imagine all the credit and goodness that gets associated with the Saint – and that's after he's been dead and buried.

So then what about us? Can we spread a little cheer? Can we laugh off some things and imagine a better outcome? Can we use joy and wonderment to alter someone's outlook or change the direction of a situation? What do the people around you need? More reality? More stress? Less possibility? Less creativity? Or maybe – just maybe – do we all need to reconnect with the childhood faith inside of us that believes in all things and spreads the word that "all things are possible with God."

Epilogue

As we consider all that the world has endured in 2020, the attraction and necessity of new approaches becomes abundantly clear. What stories or messages inspired us and gave us hope during a world-wide "shutdown"? Stories of joy, of sacrifice, of imagination... stories that excited the human capacity towards love, unity and fraternity. Against unspeakable odds, charity and concern for neighbor were highlighted and heart-warming.

At the same time, when protest and outrage sparked across the globe around issues of injustice and conversations raged around broken and antiquated systems, a deep and legitimate yearning for restorative and renewing actions was expressed. For the most part, the world remains unsatisfied as calls for change and fraternity fall flat against a world saturated in relativism and the obsession with the "self". Real change seems hijacked by a crashing sound of disconnected interests and methods. In a world where words have lost meaning, speaking out for change, but against violence seems to be unanchored from the heroic voices from the past.

In the midst of all this turmoil – the child has been forgotten. Nearly all major decisions have been made without consideration for what is best or most hopeful for children and their futures. Since they have no voice, power or platform to respond with violence, they remain marginalized and are becoming a generation deeply at risk. The same could be said for the extreme poor who suffer the most from economic recession and forced lock-downs.

Against the backdrop and the rapid pace of global change, we see the figure of St. Nicholas and the legacy of his life – lived in faith. In truth, the world changed more in his life that it will in ours. He knows about change. His joy and charity and his miraculous ability to work wonders came from his connection to the Holy Spirit. The courage and wisdom that Nicholas possessed was not his own – but was the substance of the Divine Son of God living in his life. Sainthood is about connection. Nicholas was simply living the life of Jesus Christ embodied in the 4th Century in the life and body of a Bishop from Myra. When that life "fleshed out" – the world discovered a man who was committed to generosity, children, truth, justice and joy.

What about you?

Look at that list again – think about your own life and your connection. What are you connected to? Where do you get your wisdom, your courage, your strength? Are you connected to the Divine Life of Christ? As the world changes around you and your family – what will bring you more purpose comfort and meaning: praying together with the saints and angels at Mass this weekend, or a return to the frantic pace of town soccer and lacrosse? What will bring you and your family more peace and direction – spending time together working for justice through charity or working overtime to buy the latest gadget?

Consider the yearning of today's world. What if a group of people of Faith lived their lives generously – devoted to children, the pursuit of Truth, working actively for justice – especially for the poor – and did it all with a spirit of joy and imagination?

Is that not what the world is looking for? Is that not the possibility of "thy Kingdom come, they will be done on earth as it is in Heaven"? Is that not Jesus – incarnate once again among us?

Made in the USA
Monee, IL
29 October 2021